www.LindySellers.com

Tennessee River Press

From Farm to Market

Stories of Farmers & Artisans in the Carolina Piedmont

Text & Photography
by
Lindy Mayberry Sellers

Dedication

For Chris—the one who has supported all of my wild ideas for 27 years.
And to my children- Nate, Wesley & Lainey; three of the brightest stars in my own little sky.

Contents

Foreword

Initially, the reason for writing this book was to inspire—to inspire you, dear reader, to be innovative and have fun earning money by growing things to eat or making things by hand to sell at farmers markets.
After interviewing the people for this book, its purpose has become so much more. Having the privilege of sitting and listening to the reasons why these people farm or create has given me a new perspective.
I came away from each and every interview with a new sense of pride and respect for the families that produce the items that they bring to the market. They are all so passionate about what they do, and passion is a must because it is hard work!

There are just a few things that people truly need in life: to love and to be loved, and to be heard.

I listened. Now it is time for everyone else to hear too.

Acknowledgments

I would like to thank all of the wonderful farmers and artisans who quickly said "yes" to being interviewed for this book. You all shine with such a bright light, and it was such a privilege to get to know you.

I would also like to thank a few friends who are always there to encourage a girl when she needs it most—Lorie Hedrick, Christina Parker Brown, Christy Bordeaux, and Tracy Watson—you ladies rock!

Introduction

It was late summer. I was in college and had just bought my first car. Most teens my age would have made a beeline for the mall, a movie, or a friend's house. Not me—my destination was the newly opened Knox County Regional Farmers Market.

Knoxville, Tennessee opened the doors of the market in 1992, and I could not wait to get in there and meet the farmers. You see, I have always been intrigued by farming and growing things. I guess my parents' subscription to *Mother Earth News* when I was small must have been an early influence.
The building used to house the market was huge and filled with fruits and vegetables as well as crafts, fried pies, and a variety of tasty treats. After making my purchases of tomatoes and corn, I rounded the corner to find a sign that read "Cruze Dairy," but let me stop there for just a minute.

As a little kid, my father would tell my brother and me wonderful stories about his growing up in Nashville, Tennessee in the 1950s. He told us about milk being delivered to his door by the milkman and how when they pulled the little foil top off the glass bottle of milk, a heavy, thick cream would be stuck to it. He said that he or his siblings would lick the cream off the lid and then dip their spoons down in the bottle, pulling up a big spoonful of cream. These were the days before homogenization, so all of the cream rose to the top. He explained that the milk was so rich that you could see the separation of the milk and cream through the glass bottle.

I have always loved rich foods so imagining that creamy top was intoxicating to me. I wanted to experience that delicacy so badly, but the closest I could ever get was drinking half and half out of a paper carton—it just wasn't the same.

Back to Cruze Dairy—as I rounded the corner and saw the dairy sign, a vaguely familiar sight caught my eye. There in the cooler were half-gallon jugs of milk with the cream floating big and heavy on top. I could not believe it! There in front of me was what I had only seen in my imagination.
I bought a jug and took it home. Anticipating creamy goodness, I screwed off the plastic lid and dipped my spoon down in to the thick cream ... Honey, it was every bit as wonderful as I thought it would be . . . maybe even better!

That's when the farmers market stole my heart.

Drive through most any town on a summer Saturday morning and you are sure to find a farmers market. Whenever my family visits any new town, I check to see where the local markets are in the area and make sure that we stop and take in the local fare. We have visited many farmers markets like in Dallas, Texas where we bought some of the most fragrant tuberoses I have ever smelled; the Bird-in-Hand Market in Pennsylvania where we bought shoofly pie; and the Nashville Farmers Market where my great uncle Tom sold his homegrown vegetables many years ago.

I have been involved with farmers markets as a patron and/or vendor for 24 years. I sold my handmade soaps, honey from my hives, and homemade salsa at the Shreveport Farmers Market in Louisiana and currently sell an assortment of handcrafted goods at the Locust Farmers Market in North Carolina. During this time, I have had the privilege of meeting many wonderful people and hearing their fascinating stories of how or why they became vendors.

Everyone has a story, and if you sit with another soul and listen long enough, they are usually happy to oblige you with the telling of theirs. And that is exactly what I'm sharing with you in this book—the stories of farmers and artisans whom I've met over the years in farmers markets in the Carolina Piedmont.

This book is short and sweet by design. I did that so that you could easily read it in one sitting and spend some thinking about it. So many folks don't have the time or will to read for long, and most books are not read all the way through. I wanted you to be able to finish this book, ponder on it, and, hopefully, be inspired to go out to the markets and get to know your local farmer.

Sit back and enjoy the stories from farmers and artisans who sell at farmers markets in the Carolina Piedmont.

Mary and Ray Tarlton
Windcrest Farm
Monroe, North Carolina

It was while looking for acreage for her horses in 1978 that Mary Roberts Tarlton found and purchased 13 acres of land in Monroe, North Carolina. She never expected that the land would eventually turn into a business that would supply growers with organic plants and restaurants with organic produce, but that's exactly what Mary achieved.
The land was originally a soybean farm, but ten years ago she started growing heirloom tomatoes and wanted to grow them organically.

"Certified Organic" is not an easy label to come by. Meticulous records must be kept and stringent rules must be followed to earn that distinct label. Mary's background in technical documentation, writing manuals and procedures, as well as project management, has been a big help in her receiving and keeping the "Certified Organic" seal. Mary Tarlton's Windcrest Farm is one of only five "Certified Organic" farms in the Charlotte region.

Mary has to keep track of *every single thing* she does with her plants, fruits, and vegetables. She has to write down when she seeds, waters, and feeds everything. “So that every plant and fruit has traceability,” Mary explained.

While Windcrest Farm’s original core business was to supply gardeners in the area with “Certified Organic” plants, it eventually grew into selling organic produce.

The work involved in growing that much produce is demanding, but the work involved in keeping the “Certified Organic” seal can be even more overwhelming. When I asked Mary why she did it, she answered, “It doesn’t make sense to me to put a weedkiller on something that you put into your mouth—that’s why I do it.”

Mary gave me the tour of her farm in her golf cart, outfitted with the cutest eyelashes on its headlights. She showed me her two greenhouses and five grow tunnels that her husband, Ray, constructed.

With a twinkle in her eye, she told me how Ray, a contractor, was known as “MacGyver” on the farm because of his penchant to make or fix anything. She confessed, “Without Ray, this place wouldn’t be because I can’t build grow houses.”

This seems to be a theme with farm families: an adoration and deep appreciation of a significant other who helps out on the farm. Whether it’s in helping with the harvest, tilling up the soil, or building grow houses, work is lessened when it is shared, especially with someone you love.

A sampling of what is grown at Windcrest Farm includes tomatoes, pepper, herbs, asparagus, flowers, baby ginger, and turmeric.

Ginger is Windcrest Farm’s most popular product. Mary reported, “The popularity of the ginger and turmeric has grown eight times as much as it was the first time we planted five years ago.” In October, the farm hosts a Ginger Harvest event. Folks can come out when it is harvest time and breathe in the deeply aromatic fragrance of the ginger root when it is dug from the earth. Fresh ginger tea is sampled, and the event makes for a wonderful, autumn afternoon outing.

Windcrest Farm's organic produce can be found at Matthews Community Farmers Market.

www.windcrestorganics.com

*after our interview, I saw the most curious sight. Beautiful water droplets were formed on the leaves of every one of the tomato plants. (see picture, bottom right) Mary explained that it was the evaporation of water into the atmosphere from the leaves of the plant, and that it is called Transpiration. Essentially, plant sweat. I couldn't help myself; I tasted the water and it had a faint flavor of tomato.

Mary's record book.

Transpiration of a tomato leaf.

Black Bean Soup

4 cups black beans
1 gallon water
1 ham hock
1 cup diced red onion
1/2 tablespoon ground black pepper
1/2 tablespoon salt
1 tablespoon cumin
1 tablespoon garlic
1 tablespoon tobasco sauce

Add 4 cups of black beans to 1/2 gallon of water. Trim meat from hocks and dice; place meat and hocks in stock pot and add remaining ingredients.
Cook on medium high heat, stirring frequently for two hours.
At remaining water and cook until beans are soft.
Remove hock bone and stir with a wire whip.
Serve with hot cornbread and a dollop of sour cream.

-recipe submitted by L.M.Sellers.

Dan and Meg Kypena
Middle Ground Farm
Monroe, North Carolina

Dan Kypena is a dynamo. If you were ever in a *Hunger Games* scenario, Dan is the man you would want on your team because he can do just about anything. Canadian born, Dan has not always been a farmer. He was a mortgage broker in Buffalo, New York. In 2010, he started becoming concerned with the way our food was processed. After reading and researching, he made a bold move and left his corporate job, sold the family house, bought acreage, and started homesteading. He was able to grow vegetables and raise meat to feed his family. After experimenting with grow tunnels, he quickly realized that he could produce more food than his family of three—his wife, Meg, and their daughter, Jessie—could eat, so they started selling their produce at a farmers market.

A few years ago, the family was faced with a life-changing event. The company Meg worked for moved their headquarters to Charlotte, NC. The family had to make a decision: stay in New York and Meg would look for another job, or move to the Carolinas. Once they decided to move, wasting no time, the Kypenas found a new home and land in Monroe to call their homestead.
Dan shared, “The neighbors here have been so good to us and so helpful. We are very fortunate to live out here.”

When I went to Middle Ground Farm for our interview, I was struck by the beauty of the place with its rolling hills, large pond, grasses blowing in the breeze, and very happy animals. If you are a meat eater, this is how you want your meat raised.

Jessie and one of their rabbits.

Handpainted barn door art.

The animals are treated so humanely with plenty of fresh grass to wander around on and lots of water and sunshine. Nothing resembled a feedlot here.
Quoting Joel Salatin, the American farmer, lecturer, and writer, Meg said,"Everything here has a happy, healthy life, and one bad moment."

Along with the chickens raised for meat and eggs, the Kypena family also raises pigs and rabbits. They practice animal rotation in their pastures to ensure that they are good stewards of the soil and that the animals have plenty of fresh green grass to graze on.

The amount of work that has to be done with the caretaking of the animals as well as 30 acres might seem exhausting to most, but Dan has more energy than most. Jessie, their daughter, helps out on the farm too, gathering eggs, watering the animals, and moving temporary fencing.
Dan not only raises the animals, he also renders lard from the pigs, makes his own bone both, and cans meat and vegetables.

Meg says about their place, “It is cheap therapy to me; I can come home from a rough day at work, put on my muck boots, and go out there with the animals. After fifteen minutes with them, I feel good again.”
Living this kind of life is not for a dabbler. You have to have it in your blood. There is no doing it halfway; you have to have a passion because the sheer amount of work involved will wear the average person flat-out. Dan has that passion, as well as a generous and giving heart. As Dan tells it, “I just want to eventually have this entire acreage covered with gardens, fruit trees, and meat animals. I want to be able to feed a lot of families with what I grow out here. I want to give back to my neighbors who have been so good to us.”

Speaking earlier in our interview about the soup stocks, lard, and broths that he cans, Dan said he doesn’t just give those things to anyone because not everyone appreciates the effort that goes into the making of them. “You don’t just give something like that to someone who doesn’t get it.”

When we parted, he gave me a gift of pickled garlic scapes that he grew and canned himself. “You get it,” Dan told me.

Yes, indeed, I do, and I get that the world is a better place with folks like Dan, Meg, and Jessie Kypena in it.

Middle Ground Farm can be found at the Matthew Community Farmers Market.

www.middleground.farm

Bacon, Onion, Apple Rabbit

1 Middle Ground Farm Rabbit
2 Apples
2 Onions 6 Strips Bacon (or as much as you want)
1 1/2 Cups stock (chicken, vegetable or beef)
1/4 cup butter or lard
1 tbsp. all-purpose seasoning
1tsp salt (optional, and pink Himalayan is best)
Directions:
pre-heat oven to 375

quarter rabbit, set it aside
cut uncooked bacon into 1 inch pieces
chop onions
peel and chop apples
in a Dutch oven (or something similar), sauté the bacon and onion in butter.
when the bacon is done, add stock, let simmer
add the quartered rabbit (not layered, give the guy some room)
sprinkle all -purpose seasoning and salt
add chopped apple on top
cook at 375 for 75 minutes
let rest for 5 minutes, check for doneness(just like chicken, no pink!)
remove from dutch oven, cover with tin foil until you're ready to serve
turn the stock into gravy with a little flour or leave as au jus.

*We recommend rabbit served with fresh sautéed organic vegetables, basmati rice and white wine.

*Recipe submitted by Meg Kypena.

Steve and Dora Efird
All Seasons Farm
Albemarle, North Carolina

Steve and Dora Efird are living proof that hard work never hurt anybody. In fact, I'd go so far as to say that daily physical activity and sweat are good for you. Steve and Dora look and act much younger than their calendar age.

Steve is one of the most hard-working men that I have ever met. At the tender age of 10, Steve started working for a man who would eventually become his father-in-law. This was back in the days before fully automatic combine harvesting machines. He rode on the back of an early combine harvester and filled a grain sack full as it was harvested, tied it off, and tossed it into a pile. Most bags weighed 120 pounds apiece. Hard work for a 10-year-old boy, that's for sure. As a teenager, he went on to work for a factory in Albemarle that made carpets for vehicles, sometimes working 100 hours a week. That is until the labor board caught on and made him stop.

The Efirds have not always been farm market sellers. Dora worked for the phone company, and Steve had his own wholesale nursery business for 40 years. "After the economy started going sour back in 2008, folks were not interested in buying trees and shrubs," explained Steve, "so I quit the nursery business and retired." Four years ago, the Efirds decided a way that they could earn extra income was by doing something they already knew how to do well—grow food.

Steve and Dora live and farm the land that their grandfathers worked before them. Their sons and their families, as well as Dora's mother, live within a mile of each other. They have a closeness and kinship that harkens back to the old days when families did not live across the country or move thousands of miles away for a job. They all help out when needed and have a bond that is golden.

White Eggplant (Casper)

Red Cabbage

It warmed my heart that this wonderful, hard-working family would take the time out of their Sunday to show me around their family homestead, all while telling me about their lives.

On that beautiful, sunny Sunday afternoon, Dora proudly showed me her larder in the basement. It was filled with vegetables and fruits from their garden that they canned and meats that Steve or one of their sons hunted in the past year. Dora shared, "I only have to go to the store to buy paper products."
To see the amount of land that the Efirds farm is almost overwhelming. It gave me a new respect and admiration for this wonderful couple.

Sometimes, you will drive by gardens that are unkempt and full of weeds (or maybe that is just mine . . .). The rows of corn, beans, tomatoes and cabbages at the Efird Farm were pristine and weed-free.

While touring their gardens, they drove us over to visit Dora's mother, Ms. Ethel. In Ms. Ethel's yard, the Efirds also grow raspberries, blueberries, and blackberries. They also have a brand-new hot house that was just built last year, so they can get a head start on the growing season.

Steve and Dora are a super team. When Steve digs a hole, Dora is right behind him, ready to put in a tomato plant. When a row of beans is ready to be harvested, they are there, side by side, picking those beans together.
Somehow, the love that is shown in that home makes their vegetables taste even that much better than something grown and harvested on a factory operation, hundreds, or even thousands, of miles away.

Cucumbers ready for pickling.

Home grown tomato.

Depending on the season, All Seasons Farms grows and sells a large variety of produce such as tomatoes, lettuce, swiss chard, squash and cucumbers. All Seasons Farms produce can be found at the Locust Farmers Market, Stanly County Farmers Market, Stanly Commons Market, and the Mt. Pleasant Market.

Squash Relish

2 quarts chopped squash
2 medium onions (chopped)
3 medium bell peppers (chopped)
1 large jar pimento (drained)
Mix above together and let stand for 1 hour and then drain.

Combine and pour over vegetable mixture
3 cups sugar
2 cups vinegar
1 Tablespoon salt
2 teaspoons celery seed
2 teaspoons mustard seed
½ teaspoon turmeric
2 teaspoons corn starch

Bring vegetables and vinegar mixture to boil and let simmer for 5 minutes.
Pour in jars and seal. (This recipe may be processed in the water bath method for 15 minutes)

-recipe submitted by Dora Efird

Ethel Dennis
Albemarle, North Carolina
All Seasons Farm

While 84-year-old Ethel doesn't actually go to the market and sell produce, she is a big help to her daughter, Dora, and son-in-law, Steve, and was such a treasure to talk to I had to include her in the book.Ethel lives very close to the same land on which she was raised. Married at 15, she bore all three of her children before the age of 20.

Like many others of her generation, she knows what it is like to work hard and attributes that, along with eating things out of her garden, to her great health and long life. She takes no medication and discloses, "My doctor said I was the healthiest person he's ever cared for."

While her husband farmed, she made extra money by selling milk, butter, eggs, and by babysitting neighborhood children.

When her youngest child went to school, Ethel went to work at United Mills in Mt. Gilead, North Carolina. After sewing commercially for the mill for 15 years, she decided to open up her own home sewing room where she employed several ladies and made 100 dresses a week. "That was when polyester was so popular," Ethel reminisces. "I had one lady who ironed, one who sewed, and one to do the remaining hand work. It was a very good operation, and ladies would come from all over to buy dresses from me."

Unfortunately, that all changed for Ethel's business, as well as many other small businesses in the area, when the big box store came to Albemarle. "My business went out after they came to town," Ethel told me.
Not being one to sit idle, she went to work at a local fish house and was employed there for nearly 30 years, all the while coming home from that job to work in the garden, can or freeze the abundance of produce, and do church work.What prompted me to put Ethel's story in the book was how she processes persimmons for her daughter, Dora, to sell to at the farmers market.

Ethel has three large persimmon trees in her yard, and every fall, she takes several yards of her polyester fabric (leftover from her sewing days) outside and lays it under the persimmon trees. When the persimmons fall on the fabric, she gathers them up, washes and checks them for bad spots, and brings them in the house for processing.

After mashing the persimmons through a well-loved strainer, she gathers up the pulp in two-quart bags and freezes it. Ethel said, “Most folks don’t want to bother with ‘simmon [sic] pulp, so they just buy it from me or come to the farmers market and buy it from Dora and Steve.”She is also well-known for her homemade pies. Pecan, apple, and sweet potato are her specialties, and she also makes a delicious persimmon pudding. Folks from the community know her well and come by often to purchase one of her tasty treats.You can find Ethel Dennis’ persimmon pulp in the fall of the year at All Seasons Farms.

Persimmon Pudding

2 cups Persimmon pulp
1 1/2 cups sugar
3 eggs beathen slightly
2 cups flour
1 cup milk
1 tsp. vanilla
1 stick margarine. melted

Blend all ingredients. Put in ungreased baking dish (9x13 or 2 pie pans) Bake at 350 degrees for 30 minutes.

-recipe submitted by Ethel Dennis

Homer and Wadine Taylor
Black and Blue Farm
Oakboro, North Carolina

Homer Taylor has been farming all his life, and most of it was done on his granddaddy's farm, adjoining the land that he now owns. He picked everything from corn to cotton as a boy, and now he grows varieties of blueberries, blackberries, and grapes, along with many heirloom vegetables, such as green beans, purple hull peas, tomatoes, corn, butterbeans, cornfield bunch beans, and so much more. Homer has been married to Wadine for 47 years, and they have raised two children.

A contractor by trade, Homer started his four-acre garden as a hobby but quickly realized that he could grow more than the family could eat, so he started selling at the farmers market.

It was a hot June evening when I visited the Taylor family farm. Homer and Wadine gave my daughter and me the grand tour of their nearly 30 acres. We started out in the blueberry patch and walked over to the area where they grow watermelons.

Their land looks like a park because everything is so well kept. There is a big pond on the property that the Taylors use to irrigate their gardens with a system that Homer put in himself. Additionally, the pond, filled with fish, makes for a captivating spot to sit and relax.
While we were standing there, taking in the beauty, Homer told of the many fox holes that were dug out on the land and how he and his brother used to play in them as children. He told me that they would spend hours playing in them, and many times, they would find old knives, coins, and other relics from years past. Apparently, Homer explained, during World War II, the land was used for maneuvers for soldiers getting ready to be sent overseas. Young enlisted men would come to Oakboro where they would train for the war. While they were sitting in those fox holes, the contents of their pockets must have fallen out. I found myself thinking of how heartbreaking it was to know that some of the owners of those old treasures never returned home.

The Taylors have an abundance of blackberries and blueberries planted on their farm that they use to make their own wine. The blackberries are bigger than a man's thumb, and the blueberries are sweet and grow in profusion. I had the opportunity to sample some of that homemade wine at the end of our tour. And let me tell you—it was the perfect cold refreshment after walking around in the heat.

After seeing all of the berry vines, we rounded another bend where Homer stopped us to tell another story.

"A hundred and fifty years ago, there lived a family in a little log cabin, right up here on this hill. One afternoon, the skies grew threatening, and the wind began to howl. The mother called to her children to get in the cabin quick, a tornado was coming! Unfortunately, the mother and her two children died in the twister. Many years later, a neighbor was up there picking cotton when the skies turned dark, yet again. The neighbor, clear as day, heard a mother's voice calling out for her children, but when he looked up, he could see no one there."

I love a good ghost story, and that one sent chills down my spine.

It is notable how much things have changed in Homer and Wadine's lifetime. Homer told me that he was one of the last of his generation alive who lived as he had as a child.

Oakboro had been very rural when he was growing up. Homer and his family picked cotton by hand and drove it, on the bed of a mule-powered wagon, to town. This was during the 1950s. They would tie the mule up to the hitching post and take their cotton to the gin. Afterwards, the money made by the cotton would pay for all of the shoes, clothing, and books for the children for the school year.

Those were some very hard-earned shoes.

He also told of camping out in the woods near his home with his brothers and cousins in a tent that he bought using the money he earned from selling subscriptions to the magazine, *Grit*. It's delightful how that magazine has earned many country children their playthings through the years. I remember my grandmother telling me how she bought a Shirley Temple doll from the earnings she received from selling *Grit*. Check it out sometime. It has been in publication for 125 years.

The last part of our tour brought us back up to the house for a look at the arrowhead collection. The amount of Native American artifacts that Homer has collected on his land is magnificent! He has at least ten (maybe more) display cases of carefully arranged arrowheads and other tools that the Indians once used.

Spending a few hours with the Taylors on their farm made for such a refreshing evening. As we parted, we were gifted with a bag of freshly picked green beans. A day later, as my daughter and I sat on our porch, breaking the beans, I reflected on how much easier we have it now, but wondered if our easy lives make us a bit soft. Hard work will make you strong and tough. Maybe we need a little more hard work and grit in our lives.

You can find Black and Blue Farm's produce at the Stanly County Farmers Market.

Super Easy Beef Enchiladas

1 pound ground beef
10 oz can enchilada sauce
1 can cream of chicken soup
1 can tomato soup
10 flour tortillas
2 cups shredded cheddar cheese.

In a skillet, cook beef and drain. Combine enchilada sauce and soups. Pour 1 cup of sauce mixture into bottom of greased 9 x 13 baking dish. Stir in 1 cup sauce mixture into beef, and then stir in 1 1/2 cups cheddar cheese. Spoon 1/4 cup full of beef down center of tortillas. Roll up tightly: place 10 tortillas seam side down in pan. Top with remaining sauce.
Cover with foil and bake in 350° oven for 25 to 30 minutes. Uncover, sprinkle with additional cheese. Bake 5 to 10 minutes longer or until cheese is melted.
This recipe is great addition to your homemade freezer meals list. Perfect in a pinch if you have unexpected guests.

-recipe submitted by L.M.Sellers.

Pat and Jay Gaddis
Fair Meadow Bakes
Mt. Pleasant, North Carolina

"Joyful" is what comes to mind when I think of the home and business of Pat and Jay Gaddis of Fair Meadow Bakes.
Anytime I have ever been in the presence of Pat, her happiness has freely rubbed off on me. Although not born a Southerner, she has quickly picked up the graciousness of real Southern hospitality with the "pizza nights" she puts on twice a month for the community.
The Gaddis family started a tradition of Friday night homemade pizza back in 1983, a tradition that I explain in more detail below. They came up with the idea because it made for a fun evening and kept their children and their friends close to home.

In 2008, after a tour of the New England states and seeing that wood ovens were prevalent in that area, they decided to build one at their home in North Carolina. A year later, the first fire was built in the oven. Pat says that a lot of trial and error went in to learning how to use the oven and getting the temperature just right.

After the oven was fired up and used for pizza, it would remain hot for days. Being frugal in nature, Pat didn't want that heat to go to waste, so she started baking bread for her family in it.

Word quickly got around about the delicious, homemade bread that was baked in their wood-fired oven. Folks in the community would start coming by and standing at the mouth of the oven, waiting for those tasty loaves to emerge.

Soon afterward, a bread baking business was born. Fair Meadow Bakes was named for Jay's grandfather's farm in New York. They even have the original sign from the farm on display.

Pat keeps everything local, and perhaps that's why everything tastes so delicious. She uses berries from her neighbor's berry patch. Eggs from her own chickens go into her baked goods. Lindley Mills in Graham, North Carolina supplies her with fresh organic flours. As Pat says, "If you are feeding people, you want to give them the best there is."

Pat and Jay now host a twice-monthly pizza night at their place where they bake a large assortment of pizzas. My children and I had the opportunity to go to one, and it was a delightful experience. Reservations are needed, and there is a limit of 25 people. You bring your own drinks, and payment is made by donation. On the evening we arrived, a huge thunderstorm appeared, pouring rain for a few minutes, cooling everything down nicely on that summer evening. A giant rainbow appeared in the sky soon afterward. It was magical!

There were three different families there for pizza, and, by the end of the evening, conversation was flowing freely.

We all exchanged business cards and parted as friends. Pat says that is typical of all of the pizza evenings—people parting as friends. How could you not leave happy, with a belly full of good food?

Fair Meadow Bakes' goods can be found at the Stanly Commons Farmers Market, the Mt. Pleasant Farmers Market, and the Stanly County Farmers Markets. They also host a Heritage Festival in the fall that showcases the fading arts, such as spinning, weaving, basket making, and, you guessed it, brick oven baking.

www.fairmeadowbakes.com

Chili Sauce

"This recipe was given to me by Jay's mom 32 years ago, it is excellent with beans, on burgers and grilled meats. Brings back a bit of summer in the winter months." - Pat Gaddis

30 tomatoes, mashed by hand
8 large onions, chopped
4 stalks celery, chopped
4 hot peppers, chopped
4 bell peppers, chopped
1 cup salt
5 cloves chopped garlic

Combine all of the above in a large bowl, let it stand one hour.
Place all in a jelly bag (or cheesecloth bag) and let it drain overnight.
Discard the liquid.

The next day, mix the contents of the bag with the following :
4 cups sugar
1 Tbsp dry mustard
1 Tbsp cinnamon
1/2 tsp ground cloves
4 cups apple cider vinegar(which has been scalded and cooled)

Bring to a boil, boil one minute. Ladle into clean pint jars, seal, and process.

-recipe submitted by Pat Gaddis.

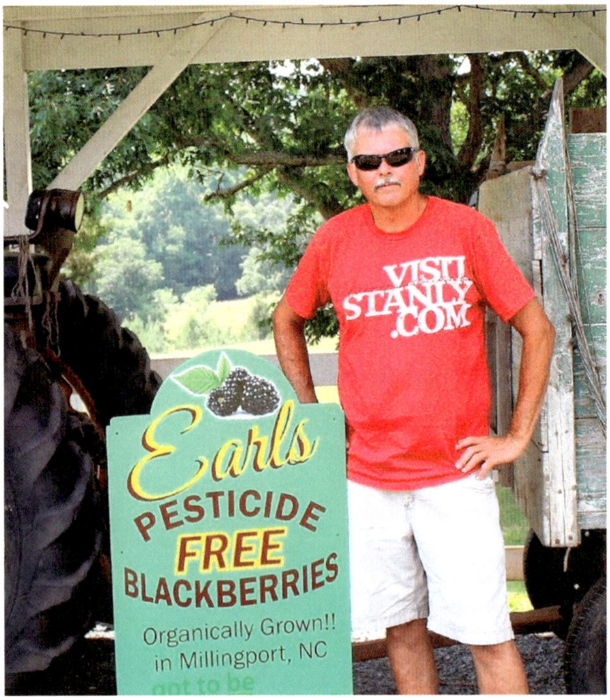

Earl Almond
Earl's Famous
Albemarle, North Carolina

Tucked in the rolling hills of Stanly County sits the farm of Earl Almond. Earl is very fortunate, as the land that he works is the same land that his daddy and granddaddy before him farmed. Farming and heritage are rooted deep within Earl, and it is apparent when you visit his homeplace.

Now, before we get started on his farming story, you know it would be unusual to write a book about North Carolinians without coming across someone who had racing in their background. Along with his brothers, for 30 years Earl built racing engines for NASCAR drivers, such as Benny Parsons, Dale Earnhardt, Bobby Allison, and Petty Enterprises. He has an incredible story to tell, but that is for another book.
The siren song of the farm was always calling his name while he worked offsite in the engine business. Whenever he had any time away from the racing industry, you could find him working the land alongside his father, but those times were few and far between.

After deciding that he had been in the business and away from home long enough, he decided to retire from engine building. He still needed a paycheck and insurance, so he went back to school for a couple of years and then landed a job at a waste water treatment plant. The hours are perfect: 6 am–2 pm. Now his afternoons are free to do what he truly loves—farming.
Earl's gardens and workshop are impeccable. Blackberries are the first crop that he experimented with, three little rows to be exact. He got more harvest from those than he could sell at the farmers market, so he decided to make the extra berries into jelly syrup and barbecue sauce.

He has quite a following in the county with a barbecue recipe that his father-in-law gave him nearly 35 years ago. Folks love it, and he caters weddings and other special events in town.

Looking towards the future, Earl explained that he had to earn a living off something other than blackberries. After consulting with the folks at NC State, it was determined that Christmas trees would grow very well in his soil and would eventually earn him a nice income. It takes six years for a tree to mature to the correct, Christmas tree size. He is projected to open the pick-your-own-Christmas-tree part of the farm in 2016. The Christmas tree farm will be an agricultural destination with a playground for the kids and photo opportunities. After you've picked out your Christmas tree, you can even enjoy some lunchtime barbeque.

Family and history are very important to Earl. He is very lucky in that he has so many family members around, ready to pitch in and help with the business. He had an old store moved to his property, and it is filled with old family memorabilia, photographs, and items used in bygone days. I could have

spent the entire time in that little store because each and every item had a fascinating story to go along with it.
To ensure that his land never gets divided and sold for development, Earl had it put into a North Carolina land trust. This will ensure that this gorgeous property will always stay agricultural farmland.

You can find Earl's Famous blackberries, barbecue sauce, and jam at the Stanly County Farmers Market, Locust Farmers Market, and Mt. Pleasant Market.

Three Meat Stromboli

2 loaves 1 pound each frozen bread dough, thawed
1/2 pound thinly sliced deli salami
1/2 pound thinly sliced deli ham
1/2 pound thinly sliced pepperoni
1/2 pound thinly sliced provolone cheese
2 cups shredded part skim mozzarella cheese
1/2 cup grated Romano a promise on cheese
1 tablespoon garlic powder
1 teaspoon dried oregano
1 teaspoon dried parsley flakes
1 teaspoon pepper
1 one egg yolk –beaten

Let dough rise until doubled, according to package directions. Punch down. Roll each loaf into a 15" x 12" rectangle.
Arrange a fourth of the salami, ham, pepperoni, and provolone cheese over each rectangle. Sprinkle each with a fourth of the mozzarella cheese, garlic powder, oregano, parsley and pepper. Roll up each rectangle jellyroll style beginning with long side. Seal seems. Place seam side down onto two greased baking sheets
Brush with egg yolk. Bake at 375 for 25 to 30 minutes or until golden brown.
Let stand five minutes before slicing.

Delicious with a crisp salad.

-recipe submitted by L.M.Sellers.

Kate Lachance Brun
Lucky Leaf Gardens
Harrisburg, North Carolina

Out of adversity comes opportunity. —Ben Franklin

The economic crash of 2008 left Kate Brun and her husband in a tough situation. They were a team in the housing business—he a contractor and she a realtor. With no one to buy or build houses for, they needed a way to earn an income.

Kate had always gardened as a girl with her father, so she decided to plant two flats of microgreens in her sunroom. (Microgreens are tiny, edible greens grown from the seeds of herbs, vegetables, or grain.) She carefully tended to her small crop until they were ready to harvest. The results were so tasty and the process so rewarding that she decided to grow even more to sell at local farmers markets and perhaps area restaurants.

The first restaurant that Kate took her carefully harvested greens to stood her up. Not to be deterred, she walked over to the eatery next door, and they quickly bought up everything she had and ordered more for the following week.
As word spread about her microgreens, demand grew. After an article was written in the *Charlotte Observer* about her microgreens, their popularity exploded, and Kate had to build a large greenhouse to take care of her ever-expanding business.

John Lachance, Kate's dad, works as a deliveryman and harvester in the business. After retirement, she asked him if he would consider moving to North Carolina and help her with the business. He told me in a great Bostonian accent, "I was retired for ONE day, and I drove a moving truck for that ONE day!

Flats of Microgreens.

These tiny greens pack a powerful flavor.

In a few short years, they managed to go from selling at farmers markets to selling commercially.
Seeing someone excited about her business and taking on opportunities to teach the community is so intriguing. Kate works with local school children and garden clubs, teaching about organic gardening and producing your own food. She plans on expanding and hosting workshops about vermiculture, permaculture, and mushroom growing.

As Kate gave me a tour of the greenhouse, she explained how it takes a week to grow a flat of microgreens. One ounce of their "Lucky Mix" has the same nutritional value as three cups of broccoli.
As I sampled the different varieties of greens available, I was amazed that a tiny carrot green tastes exactly like a fully-grown carrot and a beet green tastes just like a beet. They grow over 40 varieties of herbs, vegetables, ancient grains, and wheatgrass.
They use a locally sourced special soil mix that helps the microgreens to retain more minerals and color and to maintain a longer shelf life.

If you've never tasted a microgreen, find some and experience the powerful flavor that they pack.

Lucky Leaf Gardens' microgreens can be found seasonally at the Piedmont Farmers Market.

www.luckyleafgardens.com

Microgreen Salad with an Asian Vinaigrette:

8oz. Lucky Mix (Micro Radish, Micro Broccoli, Micro Kale and Micro Cabbage), or any Brassica based mix of microgreens
¼ Cup finely chopped celery
¼ Cup finely chopped carrot

Vinaigrette:
2 Tbsp Rice Vinegar
2 Tbsp Soy Sauce
1 Tbsp Sesame Oil
½ tsp Ground Ginger (or use grated fresh ginger)
½ tsp fresh garlic, minced
Sesame Seeds (optional)

Mix vinaigrette ingredients together and drizzle over Salad ingredients – remember, with microgreens, a little goes a long way – use vinaigrette sparingly, tasting as you add it to the salad.
Over saturating your microgreens will cause them to wilt, losing their crisp fresh texture.

-recipe submitted by Kate Brun.

Nancy Duffie
Handmade Baskets
Charlotte, North Carolina

Some people are born teachers, and Nancy Duffie is one of the lucky few who can make that claim.

Originally from the New England area, handwork has always held an interest for Nancy. She started out quilting, then switched to knitting, and then paper quilling, but felt that those weren't her niche. Her true calling came when she picked up a reed and weaved it into her very first basket.

For 30 years, Nancy has worked to perfect her useful and artistic craft. Her baskets are some of the finest I've seen. The best part is how utilitarian they are. Yes, they are beautiful tucked in a corner, holding magazines, but baskets have so many other uses. You can take them to market, use them to carry a hot casserole to a friend, or hold all of the fish you have caught. (See picture below.) She makes baskets in every size from great big laundry baskets all the way down to very small baskets to hold tiny treasures. A lot of time and work go into the making of her baskets, and the process is fascinating to watch.

During the interview, Nancy demonstrated an intricate Japanese weave that resembled a knot. The completed basket will be a work of art.

She also restores the canes in old chairs that have worn through. Not many folks know how to do this type of work, but with Nancy around, you can learn! As a special education teacher throughout her career, she loves to teach others how to make baskets. Just a short five years after learning herself, she started showing people how they could make their own creations.

"People are always so surprised at how well their first baskets turn out," shares Nancy.

After moving from New Hampshire to North Carolina in 2012, Nancy started teaching classes at the Matthews Community Center and at the Indian Trail Cultural Arts Center. She also offers basket-making classes at her home on Wednesdays, and if you are ever interested in hosting a basket-making party, she will come to your home and show your guests the lost art.

As I was leaving, I asked her how she stayed so fit. I was surprised to learn that she is a marathon runner and has completed several marathons! There are always surprises during these interviews.
Nancy teaches basket-making classes at the Matthews Community Center and the Indian Trail Cultural Arts Center.

Nancy and her baskets can be found at the Mint Hill Farmers Market, or you can contact her over email at Njbd52@yahoo.com.

Mini Tobacco Basket

Fishing Basket

Chicken Enchiladas

8- 6 inch tortillas
1/2 cup chopped onion
4 cloves garlic, minced
1 tsp ground coriander
1/4 tsp pepper
2 tbsp margarin or butter
3 tbsp flour
1 8-ounce carton sour cream
2 cups chicken broth
1 4 ounce can diced green chili peppers, drained
1 cup shredded Monterey Jack cheese
2 cups chopped cooked chicken

Sauce:
Cook onion, garlic, coriander and pepper in butter or margarine til tender. Stir flour into sour cream and add to mixture. Stir in broth and chili peppers slowly til thick and bubbly.

Filling:
Stir 1/2 cup of sauce into chicken/ Place about 1/4 cup of filling in each tortilla. Roll up and arrange seam side down in small baking dish. Top with remaining sauce.

Bake covered at 350 degree oven for 35 minutes. Remove add remaining cheese and baked uncovered for 5 minutes. Serve.

-recipe submitted by Nancy Duffie

Kevin and Julia Lowder
Peachberry Farms
Millingport, North Carolina

Way off the main road and snugly nestled on 60 rolling acres lies the home of Kevin and Julia Lower of Peachberry Farm. Their beautiful home is a restored 1925 farmhouse, sitting serenely among barns, a garden, and a peach orchard.

Kevin and Julia both have deep roots in their trades. As a boy, Kevin worked alongside his father and grandfather with hogs, cattle, and fruit trees. Julia grew up helping her parents with the family catering business and has been baking cakes since she was a girl of twelve.
Both of these skill sets help make up the business of peach growing and cake baking. Julia had a desire to be a stay-at-home mother after the birth of their daughter, Lillian. Once the North Carolina Department of Agriculture inspected and approved her kitchen, Julia started a baking business.

She bakes a variety of goods, such as pecan pies, apple loaves, mixed berry pies, German chocolate cakes, and her famous, peach cream cheese pound cakes. For these, she uses peaches grown on her own farm, so it is no surprise they are very popular among her customers! Julia confided, "People love the things I make and tell me all the time. That keeps me motivated."

Like many people, the economy collapse of 2008 left Kevin without a job. Sadly, his father passed away during that time too. He then decided that he would become a full-time farmer to preserve the family land and keep all of the peach trees from dying out.

Kevin started setting peach trees out with his granddad back in 1990. They now have over 40 varieties of peaches that are grown on the picturesque farm. Strawberries and other vegetables are grown too and are sold at a roadside stand, as well as at several farmers markets in town.
It is endearing to see this young couple work so hard to keep their family farm going and, hopefully be passed down to their little girl.

Peachberry Farms' produce and baked goods can be found at the Stanly County Farmers Market, Stanly Commons Market, and Locust Market.

https://www.facebook.com/pages/Peachberry-Farms-Bakery

Oven Roasted Okra

1 pound Fresh Okra, cut
3/4- teaspoon Salt
1/4 teaspoon Onion powder
1/4 teaspoon Garlic powder
1 Tablespoon oil (I use sunflower oil) but any oil will work
1 small tomato cut into small pieces
Preheat oven to 400. Mix above ingredients together in a medium size bowl and spread on a baking sheet. Cook about 20 minutes or to your liking.

Feeds 2-4 people

-recipe submitted by Julia Lowder

Lynnette Prichard
Mint Hill Herb Guild
Mint Hill, North Carolina

Mint Hill native, Lynette Prichard has loved learning about and using herbs for years.
With a desire to teach others how to identify, cook with, and use herbs on a daily basis, she started the Mint Hill Herb Guild in 2009. As Lynette has always grown herbs for their beauty, she now sells them at the market, so that others can enjoy them as well.

If you are interested in herbs, Lynnette is your go-to lady. She is well versed in their uses and if you are able to meet up with a group like hers that can teach you about herbs, you will forever be grateful. I started growing herbs in my backyard as a teenager and have absolutely been in love with them ever since. The guild hosts a monthly program in which a member demonstrates how to cook with herbs, their medicinal uses, and the required growing conditions.

The morning of our interview was hot and humid but not for long. As we sat on her back patio, Lynnette, in her sweet, Southern style brought out cookies and lemonade for our refreshment. Surrounding us in her well-manicured backyard were magnolia cuttings that she had rooted in pots, fragrant mints, and many other herbs that she sells at the Mint Hill Farmers Market. However, herbs are not the only thing that the guild sells at the market. They also sell baked goods and herb butters. All of the funds go directly to the guild's current project, the restoration of Bain School.
Bain School was founded in Mint Hill in 1889 and is reported to be the oldest school in the Charlotte-Mecklenburg system. Lynette was a fifth generation student at Bain, so preserving it is a project that is very near and dear to her heart. "Mint Hill needs an auditorium, and the old Bain School has a great

one that we can use. We just need to raise the funds to get the job done," Lynette explained. Restoration plans include preserving the building for use as a community cultural arts and educational facility.

The herbs and other offerings of the Mint Hill Herb Guild can be found at the Mint Hill Farmers Market, Saturday mornings, from May to October.

Basil Vinaigrette

3 Tablespoons fresh lemon juice
3 Tablespoons tarragon vinegar
3 Tablespoons minced fresh basil
2 Tablespoons minced shallots
1 Tablespoon course Dijon style mustard
½ teaspoon coarse salt
½ teaspoon freshly ground pepper
½ cup extra light olive

Put all ingredients listed, except olive oil in a blender. With motor running, slowly add olive oil until emulsified.

-recipe submitted by Lynnette Prichard

Kent and Amy Lowder
Muddy Boots Farm
Millingport, North Carolina

Kent Lowder has farmed since he was a young boy. He worked beef cattle with his family and, as he aged, moved on up to working for a commercial farmer. Armed with a desire to be closer to home and family, he started growing and selling produce from his own farm.

Muddy Boots Farm currently grows corn, greenhouse tomatoes, pumpkins, squash, strawberries, lettuce, cabbage, broccoli, green beans, onions, beets, radishes, potatoes, cucumbers, squash, and carrots.
They have 40–45 acres of produce planted. Much of it is on family land that began as a dairy farm in the late 1930s. They are lucky too, as many family members live nearby and are there to lend a helping hand if needed.

During our interview, Kent drove me around their land, over rolling hills, and through small valleys. It was such a beautiful sight to behold, with the languidly grazing cows and the field of sunflowers growing close by.

Pumpkins are grown in a field behind what used to be the old milking parlor and a stand of beehives sits nearby. The bees are there to help pollinate the many varieties of vegetables grown on the farm.

Not much goes to waste at Muddy Boots. The Society of St. Andrews in Charlotte provides gleaners to come out to the fields and pick the excess harvest, and the extra produce is given to a food bank. Last year, 38,000 pounds of produce was given to food banks by the generosity of Muddy Boots Farm. "The stories that the workers from St. Andrews tell are heartwarming," says Kent. "The folks who use the food banks are so grateful to get fresh vegetables, and we are happy to give it to them."

Rows of pumpkin plants

Bee Hive at Muddy Boots

Produce isn't the only venture that Kent and Amy have going on. They also own the Get Lost Corn Maze. It has become an annual, autumnal destination for many families in the region and has grown significantly in the past nine years. It is astonishing to see the work that goes into the ten-acre corn maze. First, they plant the corn. Then they make a drawing of the design they want to use that year. After the corn reaches a certain height, they go out and clip out areas to create the design. It is hard to wrap your head around the process, but they have it down pat, and each year, the design gets more intricate.

For the more daring folks, they turn the corn maze into a haunted maze at night. It was so fun to see what makes up all of the haunted houses, spooky woods, and vortex tunnel—in the daylight. Kent assured me, "It doesn't look so scary now, but turn on a few black lights and come nightfall, this place is good and spooky!"

The corn maze has about 70 volunteers that come back every fall to help

out. "We have a lot of fun, and it is just like a big family," shared Kent.

Muddy Boots Farm's produce can be found at the Stanly County Farmers Market, Stanly County Commons, Locust Market, and Mt. Pleasant and Union County Market. You can also buy it at their produce stand on Highway 73 in Millingport.

www.getlostcornmaze.com
www.muddybootsfarms.com

Meatballs in Plum Sauce

1/2 cup milk
1 cup soft breadcrumbs
1 egg lightly beaten
1 tablespoon Worcestershire sauce
1medium onion finely chopped
1/4 teaspoon salt
1/4 teaspoon pepper
1/8 teaspoon ground cloves
1/2 pound lean ground beef
1/2 pound ground pork
½ pound ground veal
½ teaspoon beef bouillon granules
2 tablespoons vegetable oil
1/2 cup boiling water
3 tablespoons all-purpose flour
1 cup plum jam
1/2 cup chili sauce

In large bowl, pour milk over the bread crumbs. Let stand for 10 minutes add the egg, Worcestershire sauce, onion, salt, pepper and clothes. Crumble beef, pork and veal over mixture, mix well mixture will be soft. Shape into 1 inch balls.
In a large skillet, brown meatballs in oil in batches. Drain on paper towels. Place in a greased 13" x 9" baking dish. In a small bowl, dissolve bouillon in water. Stir flour in the pan drippings until blended. Add bouillon mixture to jam and chili sauce. Bring to a boil; cook and stir for 1 to 2 minutes or until thickened. Pour over meatballs.
Cover and bake at 3:50 for 30 to 45 minutes or until the meat is no longer pink and sauce is bubbly.

-recipe submitted by L.M.Sellers.

Peggy Sanders
Peggy Sanders Creations
Charlotte, North Carolina

Peggy Sanders is a rare bird. There are some people that you meet in life that leave you with a feeling of serendipity and appreciation for life itself, and Peggy is one of those people.

Originally from Vermont, she has been selling her watercolor paintings and photographs at the Atherton Mill and Market for three years. In that small amount of time, she has been carefully studying the art of watercolor painting and perfecting her craft. Her paintings have such a dreamy feel when you gaze upon them, and Peggy says that is what she loves best, when customers see her work and say it reminds them of a dream or of days of long ago. Peggy remarked, "I like to minister to people in all walks of life with my paintings. I have even given my paintings away to people who I could tell were in desperate straits."

What makes Peggy unique is that she doesn't make her art in a faraway studio; she brings her paints and brushes into her booth at the market and paints right there! It is amazing to watch as a piece of plain, white, watercolor paper goes from stark to beautiful with the stoke of her brush. During the interview, she painted up a serene seascape—and she did it while having a conversation too!

Not only a gifted painter, she also plays the guitar, sings, and writes songs. While living in Atlanta for a few years, Peggy and her husband started a ministry for the homeless. "I would play the guitar and sing in the park," Peggy explained. "We would give people homemade banana bread, hygiene kits, coats, and hoodies. We would talk to them and pray for them. They became our friends."

Peggy also said that one of her favorite things is when children on school trips come to the market and visit her booth. She is able to show them how she paints and teach them about being an entrepreneur. She disclosed, “Sometimes, you can just see the spark in a child’s eye who wants to be an artist; those are the ones that I find small paintings that I have made and give to that child. I hope the love of painting sticks with them, with my small gift.”

As I was leaving and thanking her for the time she spent with me for the interview, she quickly went around to a box of paintings, picked two out, and said, “Here, for you.” She is one of a kind, and I left the interview with a new perspective.
Peggy’s artwork can be found at the Atherton Mill and Market in Charlotte and on her Etsy shop
www.etsy.com/shop/psanderscreations

**On a personal note, the impact of an artist giving you something that they have created does stick with you for the rest of your life. When I was 17, I went to an art fair and was deeply impressed with the work of Gatlinburg, Tennessee artist Arnold McDowell. He saw me admiring his work, and when I came back around to buy a small card, he said to me, “Pick out any one you want, and you can have it.” I was astounded. After carefully choosing just the right print, framed no less, he signed the back of it for me. I thanked him profusely and left forever changed, knowing that a stranger and a famous artist could be so generous. That picture hangs proudly in my home, along with two others I purchased from him in later years.*

Hayden Pearson's Rhubarb Pudding

"This has always been a family favorite from my childhood. My mom brought it home from a dinner with friends many years ago."
-Peggy Sanders

4 cups cut up rhubarb (1" dice)
2 tsps margarine or butter
1 c sugar
1/4 c water
Boil the above for 7 min, stirring occasionally. Pour into buttered casserole.

Batter:
2T butter or margerine
1/2 c sugar
1 c milk
1 c flour
2 tsps baking powder
1/2 tsp salt

Cream butter and sugar, add milk. Combine dry ingredients and add to milk mixture. Blend thoroughly. Pour over cooked rhubarb in casserole. Sprinkle with cinnamon sugar. Bake at 350 for 30 min.

Serve hot with vanilla ice cream, whipped cream or fresh cream.
Note: Frozen strawberries can be substituted for part of the rhubarb, being added after the rhubarb cooks. Delicious!! Good cold too, if there are any leftovers.

-recipe submitted by Peggy Sanders

Robert Morgan
R & M Farm
Locust, North Carolina

At the age of 55, Robert Morgan has experienced what most of his generation thought was gone with the passing of their grandparents.

As a child, Robert spent many summer days at the home of his grandparents in Midland, North Carolina. He would awaken at daylight to the smell of homemade biscuits baking in the oven. His grandmother baked 48 biscuits every morning, even when it was just Robert, his grandfather, and her who were eating them. Because she'd had twelve children, she was used to baking that many biscuits for so many years that she couldn't get out of the habit. They didn't go to waste though. "What we didn't eat were given to fatten up the hogs," Robert assured me.

When he was eight, Robert helped his granddaddy plow the garden, not with a machine tiller, mind you, but with mules. "That was all my granddaddy ever used," said Robert. He has stories that make you want to sit and listen all day.

Robert has been a fixture at farmers markets in our region for over 20 years. He started at the Stanly County Farmers Market and has since expanded to many others.

The top sellers that he grows are German Johnson and Cherokee purple tomatoes. They are heirloom tomatoes, meaning that they were grown before World War II. If you have never tried an heirloom tomato, you are in for a real treat! There is nothing like the deep, rich flavor!

Robert has built a smart growing system for his tomato vines. He made a wooden frame and covered it with a cattle panel; he trains the vines to grow up through the wire, therefore keeping him from having to tie up every single plant. It makes for easier picking too!

During the summer, Robert grows squash, tomatoes, corn, cantaloupes, watermelons, bell peppers, hot peppers, figs, muscadines, blueberries, and old-timey white cucumbers. The white cucumbers are rare and have a taste all their own. In the fall of the year, he grows, cabbage, collard greens, turnips, and broccoli. Robert is a one-man operation and works long hours to grow all of the produce that he brings to the market. He has one of the kindest hearts too. I have worked beside Robert at the Locust Farmers Market for many summers, and more than once I have seen him give an apple to a passing child or an extra tomato or two to an elderly patron.

He is one of a kind.

Assortment of Apples

Scuppernong Grapes

R & M Farm's produce can be found at the Stanly County Farmers Market, Stanly Commons Market, Locust Farmers Market, Mt. Pleasant, and Union County Markets.

Tomato Dumplings

"My mom used to make these for me all the time." -Robert Morgan

3 large garden tomatoes, diced.
2 Tablespoons diced onion
½ teaspoon
¼ teaspoons pepper
1 cup all purpose flour
2 Tablespoons shortening
2/3 cups milk
1 Tablespoon butter

Place tomatoes and onion in a medium size saucepan. Cook over medium heat until the tomatoes start to release their juices. Add salt and pepper. Simmer on low.
In a medium size mixing bowl put in flour, cut in the shortening with a fork, stir just until all the flour mixture is moistened. Don't overwork the dough.
Using two soup spoons drop the dough into the simmering tomatoes about 1 1/2" apart. You will probably get about 8 dumplings. When all the dumplings are dropped in, cover pan with the lid and cook over low heat for 15 minutes. When time is up, remove pan from the heat and allow the mixture to sit for 5 minutes with the lid still in place.

-recipe submitted by L.M.Sellers

Kate Suko
Campbell Creek Weavery
Charlotte, North Carolina

Watching Kate Suko work at her Harrisville loom is like watching a conductor direct an orchestra. She sets the tempo by threading the intricate machine, unifies the ensemble by passing the shuttle back and forth, and executes a beautiful piece of artwork when finished.

You have to be quick, nimble, and flexible to work a loom. You not only use both hands, but your feet as well, when you are weaving. Threading the machine takes patience, and the weaving process takes time. The end result is a true keepsake.

I was mesmerized while watching her work in her cozy Charlotte home on a late summer Sunday afternoon.

Kate has always done handwork whether it be knitting, tatting, crocheting, quilting, making braided rugs, or spinning wool. It was while she was making a skirt for a New Year's Eve party in high school that she discovered the weave of the fabric and decided that someday, she wanted to learn how to weave herself.

Fast-forward a few years, and Kate joined a Scandinavian Weaving Guild in Minnesota. It was there that she learned from the best, how to weave wool and cottons into beautiful and useful items.
"Minnesota has a large Scandinavian community, and everywhere you go, you can see examples of their beautiful weaving," Kate told me.

Kate has been weaving everything from scarves and towels to wall hangings and baby blankets for 21 years and has become quite an artist. Her work is flawless, and the feeling of one of her hand-woven scarves against your cheek is like rubbing your face with a cloud. You not only feel the rich softness of the cotton or wool that she uses, but you also feel the love and care that went into the piece.

She sells her woven beauties on her website and once a month at the Matthews Farmers Market. When asked why she didn't go more often to sell, she replied, "It takes a long time to weave something. I would be weaving all day and night if I had to sell every week."

If you would like to see some of Kate's gorgeous work or meet this lovely lady in person, you can visit www.campbellcreekweavery.com or see her in person, once a month, at the Matthews Community Farmers Market.

Assortment of scarves and towels.

Some of Kate's many spools of cotton & wool threads.

Cracked Wheat Bread

"It's not a family recipe, but a bread that I love." - Kate Suko

½ c fine cracked wheat
1 ½ c boiling water

1/4 c butter or margarine
1/3 c water
1 ½ T salt
2 T molasses
2 T honey
1 c milk

1 c whole wheat flour
4 c all-purpose flour
2 pkg active dry yeast

Cook the cracked wheat in the boiling water about 10 minutes, stirring occasionally to prevent sticking, until all the water is absorbed. Stir the butter, salt, molasses, honey, 1/3 c water, and milk into the cooked cracked wheat. Cool to lukewarm, the add the flour and yeast. The dough should have a slightly tacky but not sticky texture before the bread machine starts the rising cycle.

I use the manual dough cycle and form 2 loaves to bake a 375 degrees for 30-35 minutes. The bread-machine cookbook I have uses a maximum of 3 cups of flour per batch, which gives the bread plenty of room to expand in the second rising.

-recipe submitted by Kate Suko
Beard, James. *Beard on Bread*. New York: Alfred A.. Knopf, 1974.

Bill Logan
Carolina Artisan Bread
Midland, North Carolina

Bill Logan had early aspirations of going to culinary school and being a chef. His parents thought that he would be better off in another career path, so he put the dreams of cooking on hold to, instead, build job security in the construction industry.
In early 2006, he moved to North Carolina from Vermont to work as a project manager for a construction company—and he hated it.

Fortunately—for Bill, at least—the economic crash of 2008 ended his construction job.
I say "fortunately" because he was now finally free to pursue his dream of going to culinary school.

After taking culinary classes at the Art Institute of Charlotte, he landed an apprenticeship with a French baker back in Vermont.

Sourdoughs were the specialty, and Bill soaked up everything he could before returning to North Carolina and beginning his baking career.

Bill converted an old, 1930s toolshed on his property into a bakery. He installed a commercial oven and got to work kneading loaves of sourdough to perfection. That was three years ago, and even though he now works close to 100 hours a week, Bill says, “I love every minute of it.”

Locally sourced ingredients are an important reason that Bill’s Carolina artisan breads taste so good. His wheat is Carolina-grown and stone ground, and he purchases it from a company out of Ashville called Carolina Ground. “Their wheats and ryes are of an outstanding quality, as well as being local and organic,” Bill explains.

On Friday nights, Bill doesn’t sleep. He is up all night, making up to 400 loaves of bread to be delivered on Saturday morning to farmers markets, small food

Couche Cloth

Rye bread baking in the oven

stores, and restaurants in the Charlotte area.

“Atherton Mills and Market was the first farmers market where we sold our bread,” Bill recounted, “that was our ace in the hole when we first started, and after Cat Carter of Edible Charlotte purchased my bread and wrote an article about it in her magazine, things really took off. Now you can find Chef Ben Philpott of Block and Grinder using it to make up one of the finest BLTs around.”
Carolina Artisan Breads makes several different variations of bread, all using a sourdough base. These include a French sourdough, a rustic loaf, a focaccia, and a vollkorn, which is a German sourdough rye.

You can find these wonderfully made breads at Atherton Mills and Market, Matthews Farmers Market, Davidson Farmers Market, Newell Farmers Market, and at Reeds Fine Foods.

www.carolinaartisanbread.com

Frito Pie

One bag Fritos corn chips
1 can of ready-made chili or (homemade is best)
Lettuce
Diced Tomatoes
Sour cream
Shredded cheese
Black olives.
Pour chili over a handful of chips and bowl sprinkle with remaining ingredients.

*Makes a great quick supper for busy nights.

-recipe submitted by L.M.Sellers

Steve Young
Coddle Creek Honey Farm
Mooresville, North Carolina

Steve Young has a fascinating story to tell. When I first met him at the Piedmont Farmers Market, there was a certain spark about him that I couldn't quite put my finger on. He had shiny eyes and a voice that made me think perhaps he might be a broadcaster on radio or TV. When I sat down to interview him on a beautiful September morning, I finally found out what it was.

Steve is a native of Mooresville, North Carolina and lives on land that has been in his family for generations, near the Historic Coddle Creek Church (circa 1755), the oldest Associated Reform Presbyterian Church in the country. He has worked with bees his whole life alongside his father and uncle.
Because their land is bordered by other farms, their honey bees have a great assortment of flowers to collect nectar from. The bees can then come back

to the hives and work their magic by producing some of the finest wildflower honey you've ever tasted!

Steve told me, "We have two honey harvests a year, a spring and a late summer harvest, and we have around 70 hives."

As if the honey were not enough, Steve, ever the entrepreneur, also develops new products featuring their honey as one of the ingredients.

Coddle Creek Honey Farm also makes and sells "Mama Young's Peanut Butter," named for Steve's great-grandmother, who just so happened to be an organic farmer. It is made with all natural ingredients in their commercial kitchen, and, I have to say, it is the best I've ever tasted. I was generously given a jar to take home after our interview. After one spoonful, I was forever converted and had to find a hiding place to keep my children out of it!

The Youngs make a superb Carolina sourdough bread, so named because it has its own unique texture and flavor. Sweeter and softer than traditional

sourdoughs, the 100-year-old recipe they use came from the great-great-aunt of Steve's wife, Marla.

Their honey, handmade peanut butter, jams, jellies, and breads can be found at the Coddle Creek Farm booth at the Piedmont Farmers Market. If you need a little cold milk to wash all of that down with, you can find that too, as they also sell milk from Homeland Creamery, a small family dairy run out of Julian, North Carolina.

The business is definitely a family affair as Steve's daughter, Anna, helps with the market, as well his mother. His nephew helps with the honey harvest.

As we were winding down the interview, I asked Steve if he did any other kind of work, and that is when I found out how he uses his great voice. He is an opera singer for Opera Carolina in Charlotte. September to May, when the market season slows down a bit, you can find Steve singing tenor on stage in various productions.

Music is definitely in his soul because he married a music teacher, and he and his wife, Marla, are both very involved with the music ministry at their church.

Meeting a beekeeping opera singer was a delightful surprise and one of the many reasons I have enjoyed so much the process of interviewing for this book.

You can find Coddle Creek Farm's products at many locations in the Southern Piedmont, Piedmont Farmers Market, Broad Street Farmers Market, Kannapolis Downtown Market, Peninsula Community Market in Cornelius, and Huntersville Growers Market.

https://www.facebook.com/coddlecreekhoneyfarm

Pineapple Turkey Melts

1-20 ounce can of pineapple slices
2 tablespoons butter or margarine
1/2 teaspoon salt
1/2 teaspoon pepper
8-ounce container soft chive and onion cream cheese
2- French bread loaves, split
1pound sliced deli or chicken
1-8 ounce package of Swiss cheese slices.

Drain pineapple slices and cut each slice in half. Melt butter in a skillet over medium heat; add pineapple and sauté 2 to 3 minutes. Sprinkle pineapple evenly with salt and pepper. Spread cream cheese evenly on each French bread later. Layer bottom bread halves evenly with pineapple, turkey, and Swiss cheese slices.

Top with remaining top of French bread slice. Cook sandwiches on lightly greased griddle over medium heat five minutes on each side or until bread is toasted and cheese melts.

Cut sandwiches into thirds.

-recipe submitted by L.M.Sellers

Judy Young
Coddle Creek Bakery
Mooresville, North Carolina

Judy Young is a gem of a lady, someone whose feet you could sit at all day and soak in all of her years of experience and knowledge. Judy is the cook behind all of the wonderful breads that you find at Coddle Creek Bakery.

Judy started baking breads 30 years ago when, as a stay-at-home mother to three young boys, she wanted to earn some money for Christmas. She decided to bake a large amount of homemade breads and sell them at the Working Fingers Festival in Mooresville that year. It was a huge success and earned her more than enough to buy presents for her family. To this day, that is how she earns her yearly Christmas fund. We have Judy's generous spirit to thank for all of the delicious baked goods Coddle Creek Farms now provides.

Judy started out with sourdough breads and then branched out to quick breads. She now makes Hawaiian luau bread, a tasty blend of bananas, pineapple, coconut, and walnuts, as well as banana bread, sweet potato bread, and pumpkin bread.

During the summer months when the farmers markets are in full swing, she bakes every day in her commercial kitchen, making up at least 50–60 loaves per week. One important note: Judy does everything by hand. She does not use large mixers; it is all carefully crafted by her loving hands. (Maybe that is why it tastes so good.) Sometimes they are up all night baking, and, as her son, Steve, noted, "It's never dark at a baker's house."

Judy has branched out from the first festival that she sold her breads at many years ago and now sells at many different markets in the region. She is lucky enough to have some of the same customers that she had 30 years ago.

You can find Judy's breads at Piedmont Farmers Market, Broad Street Market, Downtown Kannapolis, Peninsula Community Market in Cornelius, and Huntersville Growers Market.

https://www.facebook.com/coddlecreekcountrybakery

No Bake Chocolate Oatmeal Cookies

"This is a no bake chocolate oatmeal cookie that I have made since high school and raised my boys on."- Judy Young

2 cups of sugar
3 tbsp cocoa
1 stick of butter
1/2 cup of evaporated milk
3 cups of quick oats
1/2 cup of peanut butter

Mix sugar, cocoa, and milk.
Add butter, bring to boil, boil for 1 min. Add oats peanut butter and 1 tsp vanilla.
Drop by spoonful on waxed paper and cool.
Never make on a rainy day, they will not firm up.

-recipe submitted by Judy Young

Lin McKay and Mike Shafer
Bar Chocolate
Charlotte, North Carolina

Have you ever met someone and just felt better after being in their presence? This was how I felt coming away after spending two hours with Lin and Mike of Bar Chocolate. After our interview, like the old song says, I was "walking on sunshine" all the way home.
These two are phenomenal!

Lin and Mike have been friends and colleagues for years. They worked together at UNC and, during that time, had always discussed opening a business together. Not quite sure of what they wanted to do, Lin took businesses classes, just to get a head start for when the time was right.

It was during recuperation for a broken wrist for Lin that the perfect business idea came to them, by way of American chef Anthony Bourdain's TV show.

The special featured a chocolatier from Spain named Enric Rovira. Lin was so intrigued by the process that he quickly called Mike to say, "Let's start a chocolate business!"

Not being ones to sit idle for any time, they quickly got to work, researching the chocolate making process, cacao beans, types of chocolate, how to temper it, the list is endless. There is a whole world of chocolate information that most of us don't even know about, but Lin and Mike can tell you. They have become experts!

After spending a week at the Barry Callebaut Academy for Chocolate in Montreal, they then headed to its Chicago location to further their education. They then came back to Charlotte and took classes in Concord at PreGel America with its five-star pastry chef series. These guys were ready

to rock! With minimal equipment to start out with (chocolate making equipment is expensive), they started practicing. After months of perfecting their craft, they cashed in their 401(k) plans and started Bar Chocolate.

Watching these guys work in their own commercial kitchen space in Charlotte was mesmerizing. Nothing is mechanized. Everything is done by hand. They use as many locally sourced ingredients as possible; for instance, the bee pollen that is used in their North Carolina honey truffle comes from Mooresville. And let me tell you—theirs was THE best chocolate that I have ever eaten! Mike explained that chocolate is as complex as wine. Just as grapes grown in soils of different regions have unique tastes, so does cacao, the bean from which chocolate comes.

Not only is it an art, it is a science working with chocolates; one degree difference in temperature can ruin a batch.
The artistry of their chocolates is unbelievable! Some of it looks like painted glass, some like works of art, but all of it is edible and delicious.

You can find these fabulous confections at the 7th Street Farmers Market at Greenman Farms, as well as at the Atherton Mill Market and the Davidson Market.

www.barchocolateclt.com

Chicken Breasts Diane

For 4 servings you will need-
Four large boneless chicken breast halves or eight small
1/2 teaspoon salt
1/2 teaspoon black pepper
2 tablespoons olive oil
2 tablespoons butter
3 tablespoons chopped fresh chives
juice of half a lemon
2 tablespoons brandy or cognac
3 tablespoons chopped parsley
2 teaspoons Dijon mustard
1/4 cup chicken broth.

Place chicken breast halves between sheets of waxed paper or plastic wrap. Pound lightly with mallet. Sprinkle with salt and black pepper. Heat 1 tablespoon each of oil and butter in large skillet. Cook chicken over high heat for four minutes on each side. Do not cook longer or they will be overcooked and dry. Transfer to warm serving platter. And chives lime juice and brandy, mustard and parsley to pan. Cook 15 seconds whisking constantly. Whisk in broth, stir until sauce is smooth. Whisk in remaining butter and oil, pour over chicken. Serve immediately.

Good with noodles and steamed broccoli and a fresh salad.

-recipe submitted by L.M. Sellers

Lindy Mayberry Sellers
(Your Friendly Author)
Sweet Harvest Homestead
Stanfield, North Carolina

Growing up, I was influenced by two publications that my parents had subscriptions to. One was *Rolling Stone*, the magazine (my father was a radio announcer), and the other was *Mother Earth News* (a back to basics, sort of do-it-yourself magazine). Today, I still love music and have been living, in small ways, the "back to basics" kind of life.

Originally from Tennessee, our family moved to North Carolina in 2005. After searching for a year, my husband and I found twelve acres with a house that was built in 1915 to call our homestead.

I had been making soap and bread for years already, so I decided to jump in and try my hand at jams, jellies, and relishes too. When word quickly got around in our small community about the goodies that came from that country kitchen, my cottage business, Sweet Harvest Homestead, was born.

Using local ingredients that we buy or barter for from friends at the Locust Farmers Market, we craft up tasty concoctions such as vanilla bean infused strawberry jam and apple onion relish. We make pickles using old-timey white heirloom cucumbers, and our bread is made from freshly ground, organic wheat berries.

Handcrafted goat milk soap is another item we make, and it is all our family has used since I started making it in 2001. There is a dramatic difference between handmade and store-bought soaps; you really have to try a bar to appreciate the difference.

Besides selling items at the farmers market, I also make how-to videos. I have a heart to teach young married women just starting out homemaking. I want to be the like the Titus II women in the Bible for them. I don't know it all, but 20 years of experience does help.

The business is a family affair with everyone pitching in with the farmers market or craft shows. Our two sons help set up the tents and tables, and our daughter helps wrap the breads and soaps.

All three of them are great salespeople, and my husband is the best support man around. He has a full-time job already but is always there if I need him in a pinch!

Sweet Harvest Homestead is at the Locust Farmers Market from May thru August.

www.sweetharvesthomestead.com

Photography Cards

Handcrafted Soap

Rum Cake

*I have been making this cake for the last 16 years. It is ALWAYS a hit. My favorite way to eat it is frozen. Yes, frozen- with a hot cup of coffee.
- Lindy Sellers.

Cake Ingredients:
1 cup chopped pecans or walnuts
1 box yellow (pudding in the mix) cake mix
3 large eggs
½ cup cold water
1/3 cup vegetable oil
½ cup dark rum

Glaze Ingredients:
¼ pound butter
¼ cup water
1 cup sugar
½ cup dark rum

Cake Instructions:
Preheat oven to 350 degrees. Grease and flour 10 inch Bundt pan. Sprinkle nuts over bottom of pan. Mix cake mix, eggs, ½ cup cold water, oil and ½ cup of rum together. Pour batter over nuts, bake for 1 hour. Cool and invert on serving plate. Prick top with knife or fork.
Glaze Instructions:
Melt Butter in sauce pan, stir in ¼ cup water & sugar. Boil 5 minutes, stirring constantly. Remove from heat, stir in rum. Spoon and brush glaze evenly over top and sides of cake.
Allow cake to absorb glaze, repeat until glaze is used up.

Chef Donnie Simmons
Mint Hill, North Carolina
DFC Café and Trading Company

After reading about all of the folks who work hard to bring fresh items to the farmers markets, I thought you would enjoy reading about someone who uses these products on a daily basis to give the folks in Monroe, North Carolina a farm fresh menu.

Donnie Simmons has had an exciting cooking education. After graduating from Independence High School in 1996, he went to work as a dishwasher at Eddie's Place, Danny's too. It was fate when the prep cook quit, and they needed to fill the position. Donnie quickly volunteered to be trained, and the love of cooking was born.

Donnie came from a family whose grandmother cooked from scratch every meal. His family always ate dinner together, eating foods that were in season and fresh out of the garden. Garden fresh foods are in his blood.

After doing an internship at Cibi in Charlotte and La Grotta in Buckhead, he went to work as a private chef for a company called Food to Die For in Charlotte. While working there, he fed many famous stars in the music industry. He has also appeared on the Food Network show, *Diners, Drive-ins and Dives.* This guy is a whiz with a skillet.

In 2015, he went to work at DFC Café and Trading Company in Monroe. This is where his heart is because he is able to have a direct relationship with the food suppliers. This is also where things get a little different; the food suppliers are not the big commercial restaurant suppliers that you might be used to seeing; they are the local farmers in the area.

Each day the farmers whom Donnie has close relationships with bring in their supply of vegetables, meats, eggs, herbs, and other tasty treats. From what is available, Donnie makes up the menu, and it changes daily. A challenging concept to some, Donnie is great at thinking of unique dishes to prepare with the supplies he has on hand. He mixes up unique combinations and delivers some of the most delicious concoctions; for example, pea salad with dried cranberries, omelets made with farm fresh eggs and filled with local tomatoes, and delicious chicken salad made with locally raised chicken.

DFC Café and Trading Company is a delicious farm-to-fork restaurant and a very popular dining destination in Monroe. If you are ever in the area, stop in and sample their unique, local fare.

Bourbon Sauce

1 tablespoon fresh garlic minced
1 tablespoon dry ginger
1 teaspoon crushed red pepper flakes
¼ cup apple juice
4 cup brown sugar
1cup ketchup
1 Tbsp apple cider vinegar
½ cup cold water
1 cup soy sauce

Wisk together above ingredients.
Use over chicke, pork, burgers or anything that needs an extra kick.

-recipe submitted by Chef Donnie Simmons

Afterword

Now that you have had the opportunity to read about some of the folks who work at the markets, you can understand why I came away from each interview with a spring in my step, joy in my heart, and gratitude for the opportunity to get to hear and then share their stories. When a project makes you this grateful, you know you are on to something right!

Do you grow an abundance of vegetables in your summer garden, or perhaps make tasty jams and jellies with your orchard fruits? Maybe you grow a profusion of flowers in your garden and always have plenty left over? If you have a beautiful, useful craft that you make by hand or if you grow extra produce, why not sell it at your local farmers market?

Whether you want to sell something, buy something, or just enjoy an interesting conversation, visit your local farmers market. And you never know, I'll bet someone—like me—will get to know you and find your story fascinating too!

Photo courtesy: Lainey Sellers.

What others are saying about Lindy Mayberry Sellers

"This book is a treasure trove of stories and beautiful photographs of Farmers and Artisans. Lindy's book inspired me as well as made me grateful for our Farmers who work so hard for us. I have a new respect for those amazing people standing behind the tables at the local Farmer's Markets. Thank you!"
-Ann McIndoo CEO / Founder of So, You Want To Write!
www.SoYouWanttoWrite.com

"Passion and respect flows on every page! Lindy loves the farmers and artisans she writes about. She's proud of what they do, and grateful to be one of them."
–Matt Gersper, Founder, www.HappyLiving.com

"This book is packed with inspiration and heart-warming themes. After reading "From Farm To Market" I wanted to head straight to my local farmer's market. I longed to hear the stories of the crafters and farmers in my local area. Read this book for yourself and you'll know exactly what I mean!"
-Sally Miller, author of Make Money On Airbnb

"I am left with a new appreciation of how I may obtain truly life-sustaining and nourishing foods, and in so doing, will connect with the amazing people dedicated to the purity of their crops and naturally/ humanly produced meats. I can't wait to set out and enjoy the rich experience that awaits me at the Farmer's Markets near and far! Thank you, Lindy for helping me understand the full meaning of what is going on behind the scenes!"
-Deidre Edwards, Author of Toolkit for Wellness

"Such a lovely glimpse into the lives of Farmers & Artisans; In her book, Lindy skillfully demonstrates the great importance of hard work and family connections."
- Irene Drabkin, Author of The Power of the Educated Patient: Proven Strategies for Reclaiming Your Health and Well-Being That You Won't Find in a Conventional Medical Office

Lindy's long love for a taste of natures best is clearly seen through this book. Whether it be her own experience or of the many farmers and artisans she interviewed, each bring a fresh perspective to selling their goods at a farmers market.
From Farm to Market not only takes us into the food these farmers sell, but also into their lives and the love affair they have with home grown food.
-Barry Watson, author of Rock Solid Relationship

57435355R00065

Made in the USA
Charleston, SC
13 June 2016